A book is like a garden carried in the pocket.
Chinese proverb

This proverb celebrates the power of books. A garden is a place where a person can escape from ordinary life. It is a place for daydreaming and for relaxing. The proverb means that, like a garden, a book can give escape, peace, comfort and relaxation. If you have a book in your pocket, you will always have somewhere beautiful and interesting to go. And like a garden, it will live on forever, and be just as beautiful every time you visit.

Rain does not FALL on one roof alone.

Cameroonian Proverb

Rain does not fall on one roof alone.
Cameroonian proverb

This proverb means that we all share in the troubles that come to our friends and neighbors. No one has to deal with problems alone. If someone is having a hard time, take the weight of their troubles as if they were your own. By joining together as a community at the worst of times, everyone can find the strength to keep going. Trouble comes to everyone in the course of their life, so we should not feel as if we are particularly unlucky or worse off than anyone else. Everyone experiences sorrow as well as joy.

The **MORE** you know, the **LESS** you need.

Indigenous Australian proverb

**The more you know,
the less you need.**
Indigenous Australian proverb

This proverb has sometimes been attributed to Yvon Chouinard, the founder of the company Patagonia. However, it is more likely that it has indigenous Australian origins. It means that wisdom is the greatest possession anyone can have. If you possess wisdom, you do not need complicated equipment or expensive belongings. You have the knowledge to achieve everything your heart might desire. And a wise heart does not desire things that can be bought. Simplicity goes hand in hand with wisdom.

When the sun rises, it rises for everyone.
Cuban proverb

This proverb is about equality. The sun gives its warmth and light to everyone, whatever their background and wherever they come from. We are all equal under the sun, no matter how many possessions we might collect or what position or status we might achieve. This proverb has been attributed to the author Aldous Huxley, but it is actually an old Cuban saying. We are asked to remember that the sun treats us all the same, and the implication is that if human beings could be just as fair to each other, the world would be a better place.

Laughter is a language everyone understands.

Chadian proverb

**Laughter is a language
everyone understands.**
Chadian proverb

No matter how different people are, finding a shared joke or a similar sense of humor will help them to come together and become friends. If you want to connect with someone, the best way is to find something that you can both smile about. It has been scientifically proved that all human beings share the same basic emotions, and that laughter is particularly well recognized as a sign of happiness. So no matter where you are in the world, a smile or a laugh will be understood.

Even a small star SHINES in the DARKNESS

Danish proverb

Even a small star shines in the darkness.
Danish proverb

These words are a reminder that you don't have to be the brightest and the best. You don't have to be bigger or more impressive than everyone else. Like the smallest star, the light you give out is important because it is *yours*. Without the smallest star, the night sky would be a little bit darker. Without you, the world would be a poorer place. You can make a difference to the world and to the people around you.

Dance by yourself and you can jump as much as you want.
Greek proverb

There are two sides to this old Greek proverb. Most obviously, it tells us that it is important to spend some time doing things by yourself, for yourself. When you are alone, you can do exactly as you please. But there is another, unspoken message in this saying, which is that when you are not alone you have to take the wishes of the whole group into consideration. Compromise is part of getting along with other people.

Every cloud has a silver lining.
English proverb

This saying means that when things go wrong, they are never as bad as they might seem. Something good and unexpected will come out of the bad. It is usually said after the good consequence has been discovered, pointing out that even though things seemed bad at one time, fate was heading towards something better. The first reference to the idea of clouds and silver linings came from the poet John Milton, in "Comus." It was first used as the phrase we know today in the 1840s.

A clear conscience is a soft pillow.
German proverb

It is easy to relax and fall asleep if you haven't done anything wrong, or anything that you feel bad about. Without guilt or remorse rattling around in your thoughts, drifting off to sleep is not hard. But if you have something to feel ashamed about, you will toss and turn and struggle to get a wink of sleep. The message in this proverb is clear – if you want to sleep well, be an honorable person and make good choices.

When one doesn't have the things that one loves, one must love what one has.

French proverb

**When one doesn't have the things that
one loves, one must love what one has.**
French proverb

This beautiful proverb suggests a very simple way to be happy. Rather than spending time feeling sad or angry about the things you don't have, you are encouraged to put your energy into the happy and positive things in your life. The words urge you to be satisfied with what you have, rather than always grasping for things that are out of your reach.

A beautiful thing is never perfect.
Egyptian proverb

This proverb is thought to have originated in Egypt, and it is deceptively simple. It tries to explain the nature of true beauty, telling us that nothing that is truly beautiful is also perfect. For something to be really beautiful, it must be flawed. When something has been loved and used, whether it's a book, a toy or an ornament, it is often flawed. A cup may be chipped. A toy may be threadbare. But the chipped cup and the threadbare teddy are loved, and their flaws give them true beauty.

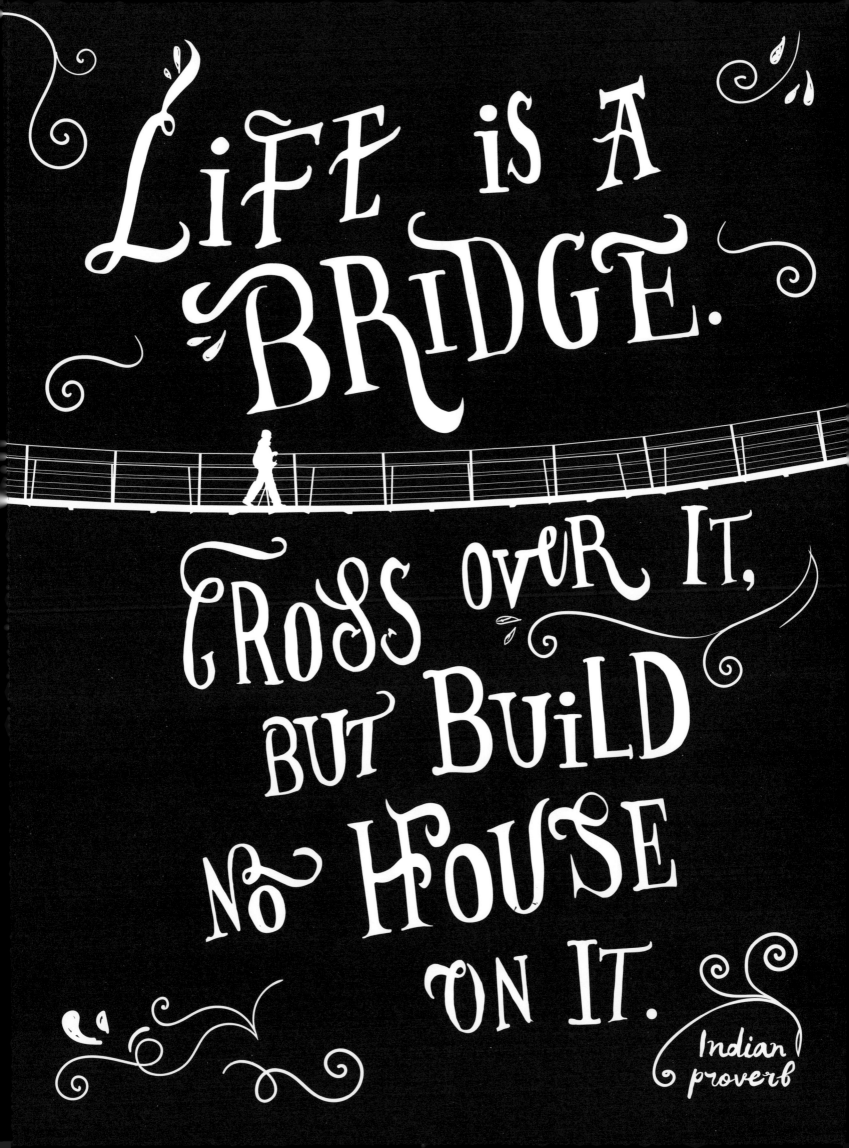

Life is a bridge. Cross over it, but build no house on it.
Indian proverb

This is saying that life is only a small part of a bigger journey – you are only passing from one place to another. Don't put all your energy into what happens here in this life. Remember that you are passing through, and have a belief in another life to come. This proverb famously appears engraved on an archway in the ruined Mughal capital of Fatehpur Sikri in India.

Swedish proverb

Those who wish to sing always find a song.
Swedish proverb

If you want to sing, you will sing. If you want to find happiness, you will find it. This proverb is a reminder that you will find whatever it is that you are looking for. No matter what happens in your life, you can choose to face it cheerfully, or you can choose to be unhappy. Human beings have a strong will and great power over their own minds. Everyone faces difficulties in their life, but if you choose happiness, you will always find something to feel happy about.

Every bird thinks its own nest beautiful.
Italian proverb

This simple little proverb means that every living creature feels attached to its home or the place where it was born. It implies that the same is true of human beings. We all think that our own home and family are the most comforting and beautiful. This saying reminds us that what makes a place beautiful is the love and comfort that we find there. We don't need to spend a lot of money and have the rarest or most impressive belongings. We just need to feel at home.

**However long the day,
the evening will come.**
Irish proverb

The literal meaning of this proverb is that even if you are having a long, difficult day, it will eventually come to an end. The evening is a time of rest and peace, and you will be able to sit down and relax. But the proverb means more than this. It is saying that even if you are going through something very hard or challenging, it will end and better times will come. Nothing lasts forever. The proverb could be interpreted to mean the opposite – that *good* times do not last forever – but in Celtic tradition nighttime is seen as the start of a new day, so the night is something to look forward to and enjoy.

**We will be known forever
by the tracks we leave.**
Native American (Dakota) proverb

When we walk, we leave footprints behind us. Those footprints tell other people where we have been and where we are going. This proverb says that in the same way, at the end of our lives, we will be remembered for what we have done and how we have affected the people around us. If we act with love and kindness, and do good things, we will leave a positive impression upon the world. If we have changed the world for the better, that is how we will be remembered.

Darkness reigns at the foot of the lighthouse.

Japanese proverb

There are several interpretations of this proverb. It may be asking us to think about the contrast of dark and light in terms of good and evil. History tells us that some of the most terrible deeds have been done in the name of justice and goodness. Things are not always as they seem, and great hypocrisy can sometimes be found close to the most seemingly noble causes. Another interpretation is that things can seem worst when they are closest to getting better. It could also mean that we sometimes lose sight of those things that are closest to us.

Turn your face to the SUN and the SHADOWS will fall behind YOU.

New Zealand (Maori) proverb

Turn your face to the sun and the shadows will fall behind you.
New Zealand (Maori) proverb

This proverb teaches the value of optimism and positive thinking. When you face the sun, the shadow you cast lies directly behind you. This proverb urges us to look toward the bright, happy things in our lives. Just as when you turn to the sun, the dark shadows are thrown behind you, so when you focus on good, positive things, the bad, negative things will be put behind you. The message is that we only do harm to ourselves by holding on to negative thoughts.

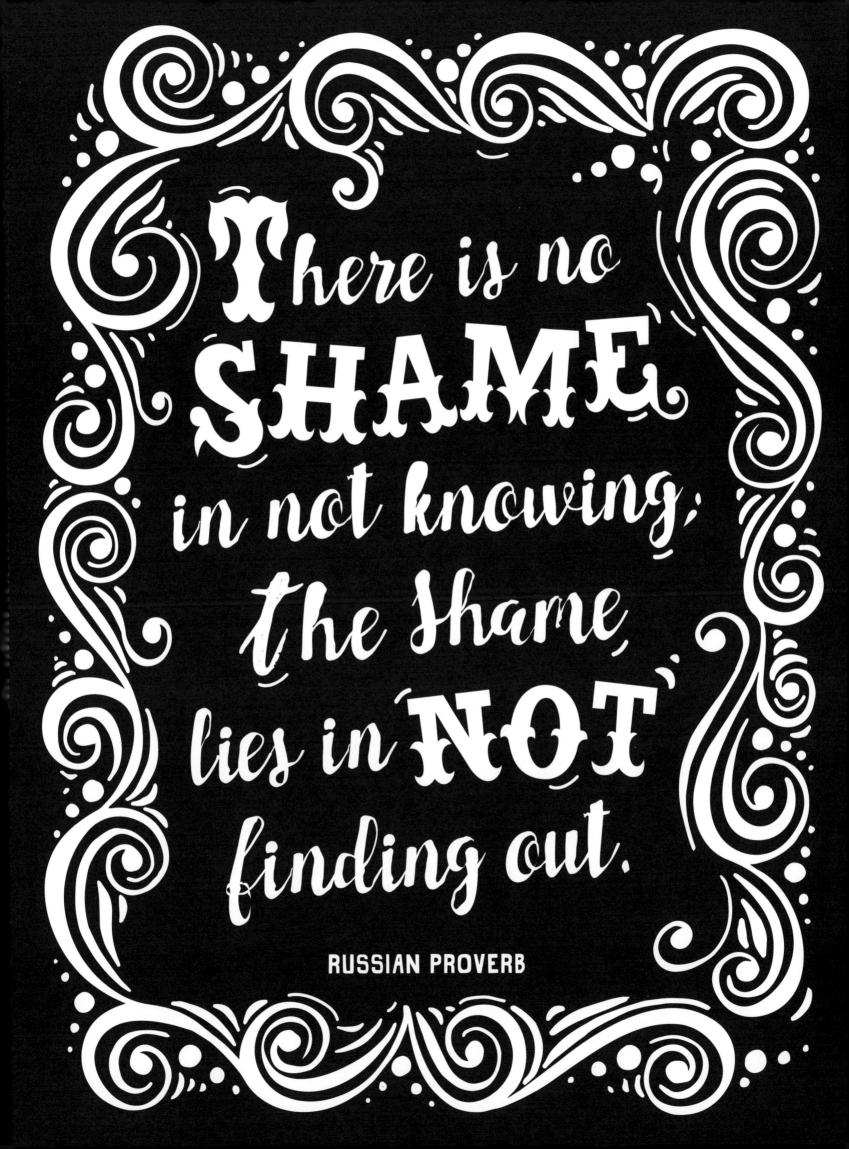

There is no shame in not knowing; the shame lies in not finding out.
Russian proverb

This is a saying that encourages learning and knowledge. It means that ignorance is not a crime, but if you realize that you are ignorant about something, you should educate yourself. When there is something that you don't understand, you should do everything you can to learn more about it. There is nobility in wanting to learn and expand your knowledge and understanding. Although this is thought to be a Russian proverb, similar sayings have also been attributed to other countries and individuals.

How **BEAUTIFUL** *it is to do* **NOTHING,** *and then* **REST** *afterward.*

Spanish proverb

How beautiful it is to do nothing, and then rest afterward.

Spanish proverb

This Spanish proverb focuses on the importance of rest time. In this busy world, one of the greatest joys is to relax and do nothing, without feeling guilty about it or having to "make up the time" in some way. Honor the time that you spend doing nothing, for this is when you recharge your batteries, when your mind and body rest together. To make a purposeful choice to do nothing is to simply enjoy being alive.

Bald people can always find a comb.
Thai proverb

This isn't really about baldness or combs. It's a wryly comical version of what is called "Murphy's Law" – whatever can go wrong, will go wrong. This Thai proverb tells us that you will always be able to lay your hands on things when you don't need them. However, you can be sure that the one thing you really need will be impossible to find!

Man is harder than iron, stronger than stone and more fragile than a rose.

Turkish proverb

Man is harder than iron, stronger than stone and more fragile than a rose.
Turkish proverb

In this proverb, the word "man" is intended to mean "human beings." It tells us that emotionally, human beings have great strength and resilience, and yet they can also be delicate and easily hurt. Physically, human beings have found ways to carry out great feats of strength and power, and yet their lives are fragile and short. This reminds us that we are all complicated and unique, and that we should take care of ourselves and each other.

Adversity brings knowledge, and knowledge wisdom.

— WELSH PROVERB

**Adversity brings knowledge,
and knowledge wisdom.**
Welsh proverb

This proverb asks us to remember that good can come out of the most difficult situations. When human beings are going through hard times, they are given the opportunity to learn and grow. As they face their problems, they expand their knowledge of themselves and of human nature. The more they understand the world around them, the more tolerance and kindness have space to grow. This is true wisdom, and it is a hard-earned attribute.

Even the **MIGHTIEST EAGLE** comes down to the treetops **TO REST.**

UGANDAN PROVERB

Even the mightiest eagle comes down to the treetops to rest.
Ugandan proverb

This proverb reminds us that every living being needs time to rest and recharge, even if they are one of the most important people in the world. Being in a position of power doesn't mean that people are above the ordinary needs of humanity. The words also tell us that no situation is permanent. Some people think that they are more important or more special, soaring high above others like an eagle, but the truth is that we were all born equal. We all have the same needs and the same human weaknesses.